Cell Phone Spirituality

Cell Phone Spirituality

✦

What your cell phone can teach you about life and God.

Kevin Goodrich O.P.

iUniverse, Inc.
New York Lincoln Shanghai

Cell Phone Spirituality
What your cell phone can teach you about life and God.

iUniverse books may be ordered through booksellers or by contacting:

iUniverse
2021 Pine Lake Road, Suite 100
Lincoln, NE 68512
www.iuniverse.com
1-800-Authors (1-800-288-4677)

ISBN-13: 978-0-595-37321-5 (pbk)
ISBN-13: 978-0-595-81718-4 (ebk)
ISBN-10: 0-595-37321-6 (pbk)
ISBN-10: 0-595-81718-1 (ebk)

Printed in the United States of America

To my fellow friars and sisters in the Anglican Dominican Order
Thank you for being my community and supporting me through prayer,
laughter, and our shared vocation to Proclaim the Word of God!

Be Still and Know That I am God
—Psalm 46:10

Contents

Acknowledgements

Thanks to Jayne and Scott colleagues in learning as well as Barbara, and Warren members of my congregation for reading the manuscript and giving me helpful suggestions and feedback.

Special thanks to my spiritual director Sr. Judy who encouraged me to start writing in the first place!

Introduction

In recent years cell phones have changed from being seen as a unique innovation to being a normal part of 21st century living. I spent last Thanksgiving in the African country of Tanzania, one of the poorest places in the entire world. While driving down dirty and dusty roads in the midst of rural fields and small huts I saw a shepherd moving his little herd of assorted animals across the road. He wore the traditional tribal robes and colors of the Massasi people and ushered the animals along with a stick. Yet what didn't quite fit into the picture was the cell phone that he was holding in his hand with which he was presumably sending a text message!

Or consider a few years ago when my wife and I sat in a pub in London with English friends we were visiting. We had planned to catch up with a friend from Ireland and were hoping she would make her way across the channel to meet with us all. One of our English friends showed up late at the pub and said "I just heard from Chris on my mobile, she says hi!" We weren't sitting in front of a computer, but in a smoky pub hundreds of miles away from Ireland. Yet the cell phone gave us instant communication with her. You and I see cell phones all of the time. We carry them. We wonder why people use them as they drive along the road and sometimes we get frustrated with them as they ring in the most inappropriate of places.

One time at our church's Saturday night service I was preaching a sermon and right in the middle of an important point I was making someone's cell phone went off in the congregation. Some people immediately frowned, and as the cell phone kept ringing the discomfort and annoyance on some people's faces grew. Finally, a woman realized it was in fact her cell phone and she tumbled through her purse to shut it off. Was I angry? Annoyed you might ask?. No, not at all. Actually I thought it was kind of funny because the very point I was making was that God is always trying to get a hold of us.

We live in a light speed world and are usually preoccupied with what is right in front of us or what is just ahead of us. In other words if we aren't focused on the present moment we are trapped in an endless cycle of thinking about the next task on our list, such as when we will have time to get the next load of laundry in. We become accustomed to zooming from one place to another: from work to home, to the grocery store, to our kid's next activity, and back and forth, and back and forth and again back and forth! After a while life is just a blur and in those few moments where we pause to catch our breath we wonder if this is it? Is this all there is to life? Well, we know it isn't, or at least it's not supposed to be, but how on earth are we to enter into that life that talk show hosts and preachers ramble about all the time?

I'm going to be honest with you and say that I don't think this book is going to give you all the answers. In fact, I'm rather tired of all of the books and programs out there that tell you that life can be explained in three easy principles and that all you need to do to be happy is to follow a particular set of seven steps. Life is more complicated than that. My hope is that this book will help you notice things differently. Notice things differently you say? Yes, think about it, most of the significant things that have happened in your life came about through a process of noticing. I remembered it was Ash Wednesday and I was heading to a class at Eastern Connecticut State University in what was cleverly named "the classroom building" back when I was undergraduate there. I noticed a pretty blonde, who I had seen around campus before, with ashes on her forehead. I remember thinking "she goes to church" and that was it. It wasn't for another year or so that I actually got to know this girl or even have a conversation with her. It wasn't for another couple of years before we were married. The path to a new life or a new perspective happens in the little things, in noticing things.

We can be in the midst of any activity from driving to shopping when our cell phone suddenly begins to ring and our attention shifts. We immediately notice the ring and then decide to ignore the call, check to see who it is, or pick it up. In many ways this is the way life works. I believe that the world we live in is far bigger, more alive, than you might think at first peek. God the great personality of the universe is always trying to reach you and me. Despite popular belief, God isn't only to be found in church, on snowy mountain tops, or during cross legged meditation. God is to be found in the grocery store, in the laughter of your best friend, and even in the middle of commuter traffic. My hope is that this book will help you notice the vast world of God's creation and God's constant call on your life.

1

This Crazy World

I don't have to tell you that this world we live in is crazy. By crazy I mean unpredictable, shocking, exhilarating, and tragic all whipped up into one world. Yet the daily experience of our own little worlds isn't always like that. At times we describe our lives as predictable, boring, and depressing. Some people would say their life resembles a modern Shakespearean tragedy others would say their life is more like a sitcom gone bad. Lots of men and women who are chained to cubicles in corporate American yearn for the freedom of an exciting job with lots of variety. On the other side of the grass there are men and women whose days are laced with thrill and variety who long for a more conventional life, perhaps even in a cubicle. Our lives are often caught in the tug of war of paradox, in the strain between opposites living together. The American comedian and actor Chris Rock expressed this idea of a paradox well when he quipped: "You know the world is going crazy when the best rapper is a white guy, the best golfer is a black guy, the tallest guy in the NBA is Chinese, the Swiss hold the America's Cup, France is accusing the U.S. of arrogance, Germany doesn't want to go to war, and the three most powerful men in America are named 'Bush', 'Dick', and 'Colon.' Need I say more?"

Maybe nothing presents the paradox of this crazy world better than television and particularly the news. I sat comfortably in my hotel in Jerusalem watching CNN. According to the reporter things were awful in Israel, including the region of Jerusalem, and attacks were taking place everywhere. I looked casually out of my window into the ancient city and saw nothing but sun, some clouds, and people going about their business. Was the reporter lying? Was I living in a land of make believe and just ignoring the obvious fighting on the streets? No, it wasn't so much about deceit as it was about perspective. If you asked the news reporter if he knew that certain parts of Israel were peaceful and serene I'm sure he would have said yes. If you had asked me if I knew there were conflicts taking place in the area I would have said yes also. Perspective is the key that opens the doors to

1

the true nature of life. What is your perspective on life? You have one, everyone does and it's dangerous if you don't know what your perspective is. As you are probably aware, one the greatest dangers we have seen in human history is when a person believes their perspective is the only one. We usually adopt the perspectives of our family, of our work places, and our society. This is normal and we can't totally get away from these perspectives but at the end of the day if we just stick to these we miss out on the big picture of life.

The World Isn't So Small After All

You may remember the classic Disney song "It's a small world after all" and be quick to nod your head that the world we thought was so large is increasingly getting smaller due to improved communications technology such as the cell phone. It would be an understandable perspective for any contemporary person to have on the world. Yet there is another perspective to be found that it is ancient, eternal, and at the same time as fresh as the morning dew. It is the perspective of the ultimate being, of the divine, who lots of people call God. From God's perspective the world that you and I live in is more expansive and more wonderful than we could ever imagine. The world that we experience isn't limited to the biological or to the useful facts of science. We dwell in a world dripping with spiritual meaning set in motion by the beating of God's divine drum. We live an existence that is fundamentally spiritual despite whatever we else we might call it.

Spirituality isn't merely about some day in the distant future when you die. Rather it is about the very breath you are taking right now. At this very instant you and I live in a world caught in a great spiritual movement of energy and meaning. As crazy as the world is, it does have a purpose and as insignificant your life may seem it too has a purpose. God the greatest storyteller of all time, whom all other storyteller's desperately fail to imitate, gives purposeful parts for the world and for you to play. These parts aren't scripted so you are more than an actor reading your lines, rather you are more like an ancient knight sent on a great quest or a government agent carrying out the most important of missions. That is the kind of world we live in and that is a taste of what life should be for you and me. Albert Einstein once wrote, "The most beautiful thing we can experience is the mysterious. It is the source of all true art and all science. He to whom this emotion is a stranger, who can no longer pause to wonder and stand rapt in awe, is as good as dead: his eyes are closed."

Spirituality has to do with the mysterious, the intangibles, that you and I experience throughout our life that mean so much. Think about the father who was a semi-professional ball player who sees his young son up at bat for the first time in little league. Or what about the frustrated executive caught in hours of commuter traffic who after swearing and honking the horn suddenly notices the beautiful blue sky and the setting sun and in that moment is whisked away from her present situation. Spirituality is about how your perspective on life integrates with your living of life. You and I usually navigate life using our own perspective but the fact is God has already established the big perspective, the big reality, and the big compass that will help us navigate through the crazy waters of this world. Religion is often concerned with ideas about God and about living while spirituality is the very living of which religion speaks about. Cell phones at there best help you to connect with other people. Spirituality at its best dials you into God, into the lives of people, and into the great melody of life in all its expressions.

The Personality of the World Beyond

I was sitting in my office at the church going through some e-mail when I overheard some people talking in the main office. I got up and stepped into the other room because the conversation was about a member of our congregation who had cancer and had just undergone an important medical procedure. I had spent a good deal of time visiting with this man and praying for him. The news wasn't very good, the cancer had returned! Sadness and frustration quickly overwhelmed me as I walked back into my office. I sat down and started to go back to my work but I couldn't. I was angry! I put my hands on my head and closed my eyes and in frustration said "Why this God? What is the point?! Help me to understand. Help me to trust you." I continued praying for this man and his family and after a while felt enough peace to go back to my work.

As a follower of Jesus I do profess to have a relationship with God that is interactive, personal, and life giving. However, I do want to make it clear that I don't have God figured out and that I can't explain why God does and doesn't do certain things. Some people talk like their perspective and God's are one and the same: page for page, line for line, down to every punctuation point. I am sold out to the fact that God does communicate to us rather like we talk to each other on the cell phone and that we can really know much of God's perspective. For my part I'd feel confident in saying that my perspective and God's are joined on a book level, most of the chapters, and maybe even a few pages. I'm not confident enough to say that I understand God on the sentence and punctuation point level.

The amazing truth is that God is interested in coming down to our level of understanding. Sometimes when I visit our church's preschool ministry I'll walk into a class and get down on the floor and play with the kids. I figure the best way for me to connect with the kids is by getting down to their level, playing with the blocks and other toys. I don't think it would be effective for me to stand at my full height, look down at them, and speak to them in fancy theological language about how God cares for them. God has taken the same approach with you and me. He is always looking for ways to come into the experience of our lives and connect with us in ways that we can understand. The punch line of spirituality happens when you realize that God is to be found equally present within the echoing chambers of an ancient cathedral and within the playroom full of scattered blocks and toys.

Getting Up Close and Personal

God is not a being who spends most of His time hanging out in the distant reaches of the galaxy or in the highest towers of heaven away from humanity. Rather, God who is present everywhere is much more interested in walking hand in hand with you during the moments of your daily life. Religion often stops at the point of concepts and belief systems about God but a religion that is infused with spirituality goes beyond concepts and brings connection between the individual man or woman and the one God. Christianity makes the claim that not only is God interested in you but that God was so interested in human beings that He became one! The Divine King became a human being so that people and God could truly be united on all levels. Regardless of whether you're a Christian or not, you probably know the name of this person who unites God and humanity in His very own identity, that person is Jesus Christ. You see before the coming of Christ very few people had any direct access to God. God seemed very far away to people even if He was active in their lives from time to time.

Over the years I've initially gotten to know some people through e-mails and instant messenger communications via a computer. Through electric correspondence and communication you can find out a lot about someone. However, when I finally met these people in person my experience of them moved from black and white to color. As human beings we are wired by design for a relationship with God. However, because of the tragedy of our world and our innate desire to choose our own way we need someone to turn on the color of our spiritual television sets: Jesus is this person. Jesus is the person who is always holding God's hand and then reaches out for yours, and if you're willing, introduces you to God. Jesus is the great cell phone tower that enables the innate ability of all human beings to dial into God to work. The very essence of Christianity is that the divine enters into our everyday experiences of making meals, driving to work, and playing with our children. This is because God, the Author of the universe decided to let Himself be birthed by a teenage girl and become one of us. If human existence were so bad, if human beings were so bad, if our bodies were so evil surely God would never have blessed all these things by entering into human existence in the person of Jesus Christ? Despite the Church's failure to proclaim this message in the past and sadly at times in the present Christianity is a very earthy, body honoring, and people centered faith. The bottom line is that God is always interested in getting up close and personal with you. So your challenge as a human being isn't in getting God to be interested in you, God is immensely interested in you! Your challenge is the same challenge that all people face, how do your position yourself so that you can notice God's presence in your life? We will explore this idea of positioning yourself to experience the presence of God throughout the rest of the book.

The Symphony of God's Purposes

You and I live in a crazy world that is difficult to understand, filled with smiling faces as well as tearful eyes, and a confusion of conflicting messages. Despite all of this there is a melody to the universe, there is a theme song to life, and the composer and conductor of that song is God. You and I have our notes to play that contribute to the great symphony of God's purposes. Yet we will never be able to know the correct finger positions on our instrument that will cause our soul to play the right notes without personal connection to the Conductor. The good news is that this heavenly Maestro is not content to leave us in the vast sea of fellow soul musicians but is interested in giving us private lessons. Great spirituality which has, throughout the centuries, given birth to some of the world's greatest music is like any celebrated song. This kind of song not only connects to the life of a lone person but unites that person with hundreds of others through their shared experience of listening to the same music and lyrics. Spirituality, which is living life based on the divine perspective will not only unite your life to God's story but it will unite you to human beings everywhere, past, present, and future.

Questions to Consider

1. What is your perspective on life? Who and what have been the greatest influences on your life perspective?

2. How do you generally experience the world, do you experience it as a big place or a small place? What makes it big or small for you?

3. Do you believe there really is a thing as Divine Perspective? Or to say it differently, a purpose to this world and to all of human life? How does God fit into that for you?

4. What has been your experience of God? Far away or up close and personal? Give some examples of when you experienced either.

5. Is the idea that God is personally interested in your life believable or not? Why?

6. What are your thoughts on Jesus being the "cell phone tower" who enables all human beings to communicate with God? Have you had any experience with Jesus?

Try It Out

Exercise #1

Take a blank piece of paper and put yourself in the middle by writing your name or by drawing a stick figure. Then draw a box around yourself that takes up about half the page. This box represents your world. Then draw arrows from the inside border of the box to your name in the center. Write on these arrows the major perspectives that influence your outlook on living.

For example:

```
+------------------------------------------------------------------------+
|                                                                        |
|    Work                                               Family           |
|  -------------------------------> Jane Smith  <----------------------- |
|    Life is about $                                  Life is about Safety|
|                                                                        |
+------------------------------------------------------------------------+
```

You will probably have many more arrows of influence than the diagram above illustrates. Underneath each arrow write the core perspective from that particular influencer. The core perspective from a particular influence is essentially the bottom line of that area of your life. By writing down the influencers on your perspective of life you will get a sense of what things are in conflict in your life and what things are in agreement.

This exercise will give you a sense of what your everyday perspective on life is. The challenge of spirituality is to look beyond the artificial box that you have created for your own little world and look beyond into God's word. The surprise is that God is right there, present in your own little world but also calling you to the greater world that He has created.

GOD'S WORLD

Work		Family
--> Jane Smith <---		
$$$$$$$$$$$$$	(GOD'S WORLD)	Safety

GOD'S WORLD

Exercise #2

Connecting With the Wider World

The trap that you and I tend to fall into is in limiting our experience of life to our current surroundings. A great way to start to broaden your spiritual horizons is take the time to notice what is happening beyond your little world of everyday living. To remind yourself to do this exercise you might want to write yourself a note, it might read **"The world is bigger than you think."** You could put it on your dashboard, your desk at work, or as your screen saver on your computer.

Every time you see your message or think about it, pause for a moment wherever you are. Look around. Notice your surroundings but then go beyond them. Imagine what is happening just outside of your building. In your neighborhood, in the greater township and from there go across the continent and finally to the stars of the galaxy. Notice your breathing and remind yourself that you are apart of this great thing called life. God who is in all these places is also especially present with you. You can do this for a few seconds to a couple of minutes. After looking beyond your surroundings say a little prayer silently or aloud, "Thanks God that I get to be apart of this great world. Amen," and go back to what you were doing.

2

Spiritual Relationships

What is the one element of any human life that if you took it away would devastate just about any person who ever lived? I'm not talking about internal things inside of a person such as their health or motivation but about things outside of themselves. Have you guessed what it would be? My argument is that this component would be a person's relationship with others. While possessions, money, and personal health might be of great value they are really nothing without relationships. What is the point of having millions of dollars if you have no one to share it with? Some of you at face value would be willing to give up your relationships for millions of dollars but would you do so if you knew that the cost would be never having any friendships again? Relationships are the meat and drink of human existence, we cannot really live without them. We were created by God as social beings and regardless of whether we are loner types, or life of the party types, we need other people. Albert Camus the 1957 winner of the Noble Prize for Literature once wrote: "Human relationships always help us to carry on because they always presuppose further developments, a future—and also because we live as if our only task was precisely to have relationships with other people."

It is no mere coincidence that we do live out our lives as if relationships were the primary task of living, because God designed human beings from the very beginning to be relational creatures. In the Biblical book of Genesis, the first book in the Bible, God creates Adam and Eve the first man and woman within the Garden of Eden. What they are to do is to be in relationship to each other, to the wildlife, and to their Creator. The divine perspective on life tells us that whatever else we might be doing here on this planet the primary reason we are here is for relationship. Religion often approaches faith from the perspective of official teachings, guidelines, and observances. Spirituality is the very relationships upon which the concepts of religion are based upon. Christianity is clear, if you intend to have enriching interactions with other people in this world you need first and foremost to have a personal connection to God.

The Essential Relationship: Don't Live Life Without It

There is a Christian bumper sticker out there that reads "Jesus: Don't Leave Earth Without Him." I think this bumper sticker is missing the point about Jesus and about life almost entirely. It is equating Jesus with the end of life and what happens beyond. What I want you to hear is the ancient message of Christianity: don't equate Jesus just with the end of life, but equate Jesus with life period. When Jesus' students were trying to understand how to dial into God Jesus told them: "I am the way, the truth, and the life" (John 14:6).

The idea of a God who runs the universe and who watches over us is a generic belief common to many cultures and religions. Many people believe in some kind of God who does something up there in heaven but is fundamentally outside of our everyday experience as human beings. Many folks want to be more spiritual and they strive to walk up the mountain of truth seeking God at the top. In Christianity, God comes down from the mountain in the person of Jesus Christ and comes looking for you. Why is this? According to the divine perspective you and I were created primarily to have a relationship with God and then to center every other aspect of our lives through that relationship. You and I were created in the likeness of God, or what the Bible calls the image of God. Our inherent hardware is designed to communicate with God and to live a life that honors God. Unfortunately, almost from the very beginning of the human story people have chosen their way over God's way.

Earlier we talked about the book of Genesis and Adam and Eve living in the Garden. Things were going quite well in the Garden until Adam and Eve decided, with the encouragement of a talking snake to step outside of the boundaries set up by God. There was a tree in the center of the garden called the Tree of the Knowledge of Good and Evil. God had blessed this first man and woman with everything they could need and want in Eden. The only thing they couldn't have was the fruit of the tree. They took the fruit and ate it in an act of rebellion that caused a major disconnect between God and humankind. Regardless of whether you believe this story literally or as a metaphor the point is clear. The unity and intimacy that was intended to exist between divinity and humanity was broken early on in the human story. If you think about talking to someone on a cell phone and then you turn the phone off, what happens? You've stopped the conversation. More than that happened with Adam and Eve. They not only stopped the conversation with God but the consequences of their actions led to the inability to have a conversation period. Their very status with God was changed. They were now disconnected from their creator. It would be like if you ran out of power in your cell phone and you would never be able to re-charge it. The battery was dead. Sin enters the world. Sin is essentially anything that separates us from God, from others, and from whom we are as individuals created in the image of God.

Throughout the centuries people have struggled to re-connect with God but with little lasting success. It was clear that humanity needed help in reaching out to God. That's where Jesus comes in. Jesus is the person who brings life back to our dead spiritual batteries so that our internal communications systems with God can work. Remember Jesus is the great "cell phone tower" that makes it possible for your messages to get to God and God's messages to get to you. Jesus is more than just a divine connection device. He is a person, He is God and human being all in one. For Christians the way to God is through Jesus.

Remember you and I were created to be in a relationship with God. God can often seem distant and difficult to understand. Jesus, divine like God and human like us, is the person who can keep humanity and divinity connected. If you want to notice the world differently you need to strive to look at it through the eyes of Christ. Starting a relationship with Jesus isn't difficult but it will take hard work, commitment, and a lifetime to develop. In that aspect it's like all of the other relationships we have in this life. But without God as the center of your life you are almost doomed to miss the point of your other relationships.

Relationships Rooted in God

Quite frequently you'll hear romantic lyrics on the radio that say things like "I can't live without you" or "I only live for you," and similar verses with like-minded thoughts. The bottom line of these songs is in a real sense, the worship of one human being by another. I'm not taking a stand against poetry and romantic songs but I am trying to point out to you the deadly mistake that all of us as human beings are prone to make. That mistake is elevating a person to the status of a god. This dynamic takes place in all kinds of relationships but particularly in romantic ones. It is a dangerous way to approach any relationship because no human being can possibly live up to the expectations of being a god. One person places all of their hopes for happiness, fulfillment, and contentment in the hands of another human being. You know from your own life or the lives of those close to you what happens in this situation. When the relationship starts to experience some strain or less than perfect dynamics the person doing the human worship will be crushed with disappointment. This pattern of going from romantic partner to romantic partner desperately searching for the "magical one" is not rooted in a healthy spirituality. Only the true God of the universe can possibly meet our soul's need for connection to something wonderful, something beyond us, and something all loving. It isn't a something we are yearning for it is someone, namely God. According to the Christian faith, we experience human relationships at their best only when they are rooted in the acknowledgment of God as the ultimate relationship. I'm not a gifted poet, but I think this poem that I wrote for my wife Melissa before we were married gives some illustration to a human relationship rooted in God.

To Melissa, my fiancée

Your eyes captured me with the most perfect silent stare,
   twinkling my soul like blue lit stars
   wrapped from God with care.
Unending joys my heart expressed
   yet to timid to acknowledge or confess.
Blessed flowers of love within my heart had grown
   realizing them I did not, until that faithful kiss had shown.
Wholeness created by the Creator is so sweet
   a half-finished painting are we, without us each.
So I long and pray for that day to be
   when heaven seals our souls for Church and world to see.
As it was in the beginning we will be forever
   a living parable of God and humanity living together.
I do, I do, I do, not once will I speak
   but with every new breath, every new look,
   and every new heart beat.
Our love cannot grow so old that it would come to death
   for it will be born anew each living moment yet.
Till in the courts of highest glory
   we are made eternally complete
Embraced by our Loving Master worshipping at His feet.

The poem expresses love for my wife but consistently acknowledges that God is the fundamental relationship that even allows our love for each other to exist. Regardless of the nature of a particular relationship, romantic or not, it must centered in a God point of view.

Sometimes you'll hear Christians say that God should be the number one priority in your life, followed by your family, and then you're other commitments.

I'd agree with this because the tendency for human beings to worship idols, an idol being anything other than God, is mammoth and has been a problem for people since Biblical times. However, I don't think the idea of God as the number one priority adequately expresses the idea of Christian spirituality for human living. The prevailing human perspective on this issue is that as human beings our complete wellness looks like a large pie. We have several different slices that add up to our total humanity and wellness: there is physical health slice, a family health slice, an emotional health slice, and even a religion health slice and so on. In order to be healthy and whole as human beings we need to have all of our slices of the pie in good shape. Make sense? This is not the divine perspective on what is required for human beings to be healthy and whole. Instead of limiting spirituality and religion to one slice of the pie, faith in Jesus Christ is placed in the center of the pie and every other area of life is flavored, is saturated, and colored by this commitment. The same applies to our relationships. It's not that God is merely number one on our relationship list. It's rather that we center all of our relationships in our commitment to God. So the Christian life always involves pondering what does it mean to be a Christ centered parent, a Christ centered friend, a Christ centered employee, or a Christ centered spouse?

Human Relationships as Spiritual Encounters

You have undoubtedly heard of Mother Teresa, the founder of the Sisters of Charity, and winner of the Noble Peace Prize for her work with the sick, the lame, and the dying. Mother Teresa often said in different ways the following: "The dying, the crippled, the unwanted, the unloved—they are Jesus in disguise." Not only do we experience God's presence in quiet places, in worship services at Church, and through times of prayer but we can experience the nearness of God through the people around us. You and I may not be in the place where we always see God in others, especially in the people who offend us, disgust us, or are different than us. Yet one of the fundamental messages of Christianity is that God comes to us in our own humanity and the humanity of others. After centuries of sending prophets and teachers God finally said I'm going to come down to earth myself. God did so in the person of Jesus Christ.

In the Christian faith our humanity is not something to be lamented as keeping us from knowing God rather it is something given to us by God. Have you ever had an experience of God in your life? When I ask that question many people aren't sure what to say. Many answer that they have never had any experiences of God in their life at all. Others say that they have had only one or two experiences of God throughout their entire lives. God is always ringing you on your cell phone. God is always striving to communicate with you. If God is in the business of seeking us out for a life changing relationship why is it that so many people say they have never experienced God at all? In part, I think this is because we bring some baggage with us to the idea of what it means to experience God.

I once spoke to a sixth grade history class about the medieval church and specifically about the life of monks. I came in the habit of my Order and talked about what I knew of the medieval church, about how one became a monk and related information. Afterwards one of the students came up to me and said "Brother Kevin, have you had like experiences of God?" I said yes and the sixth grader responded by saying "Cool!" and he looked at me like I was some sort of super hero before leaving the room with the rest of his classmates. I'm afraid this boy was probably thinking of angels, and the heaven's opening up, and voices from the clouds speaking to me. He along with many adults think of God experiences as some sort of supernatural and miraculous events that only happen to select individuals.

God has on occasion used such divine theatrics to communicate with people throughout history. The promise of the Bible and the Christian faith is that every believer would have experience and connection with God. Clearly then these divine fireworks can't be God's primary way of being in touch with His people. There most be some other ways for human beings like you and me to experience the divine. One of the major ways is through the lives of the people around us.

Have you ever been with a group of friends and been having the most wonderful time? Maybe it was on a vacation or at a small gathering on the back deck of your house. The atmosphere was just right, you felt intensely connected to everyone present, it was a moment you wish you could return to. It stands out as a powerful memory. God is in the business of connecting us to each other. One sign of God's presence is when people are in healthy community to one another.

Sometimes we find ourselves in a difficult time in our life. Maybe you've received bad news. Or you're facing a big decision and don't know what direction to go in. Then unexpectedly the right person shows up and says the thing you needed to hear. That is a God moment. That is an example of God working in your life through the people around you. God can work though all kinds people, even if they don't believe in Him, to communicate with you. So one thing to look for in your daily life are the God moments. Just as you are never sure when your cell phone is going to ring you can never be totally sure when a God moment will come your way. So be alert!

Relationships Are Life's Best Investment Plan

Relationships are what make life worth living. We can be in relationship with other people in so many different ways. Some people we relate to as friends, some we relate to as strangers, and some people we will never meet but we are still connected to them by God and by the fact we breathe the same air. As a priest and pastor I have had the privilege of being with people near the end of their life in hospitals and in care facilities. Never does anyone tell me as they approach death, "Oh I wish I had spent more time in the office," or "I wish I had made more money." By and large people wish they had spent more time cultivating their relationships with other people and with God. At funerals when I hear people tell stories of their loved ones, they never say "You know she was really great because of all the hours she put in at work," or "I really liked him because he was rich." The stories people tell at funerals are one's of friendship, love, and family. Life when it's said and done is all about relationships. Don't place your treasures in the wrong department of life. Invest in relationships because according to the Christian faith they are the only things that you can "take" with you! As you invest and put energy into the people in your life make sure you are simultaneously committed to an ultimate relationship with God through Christ. It's only through the Creator that we can truly experience human relationships at their best.

Questions to Consider

1. What are your thoughts about the Christian concept that the purpose of life is to have relationships with God and other people?

2. Do you think that our spiritual batteries as human beings are really dead? and that we really need someone, namely Jesus, to recharge them?

3. Do you consider yourself to have a relationship with God through Jesus? What is it like for you?

4. Have you ever made a god of another human being? What was the experience like for you?

5. What would it mean for you to have Christ centered relationships?

6. What do you think about the idea of God moments? How could you help yourself to be more alert for them in your life?

Try It Out

Exercise #1
Forget W.W.J.D. Think about W.W.J.S.?

You probably have heard of the statement, "What Would Jesus Do?" But I would submit to you that a better question to ask ourselves as we seek to nurture our souls is, "What Would Jesus See?" What would Jesus see in your relationship to your spouse? What would Jesus see in the person that most frustrates you or repulses you? What would Jesus see in the homeless person on the street? I can suggest that unlike many of us Jesus would notice, would *see* that homeless person to begin with!

The Christian faith calls us to be like Jesus to each other. It's impossible to say the right words or to do the right actions if we don't see the world's landscape from Christ's perspective. So keep asking yourself, "What Would Jesus See?" Make your own "W.W.J.S." bracelet if you want!

Exercise #2
Does Christ Make A Difference Really?

On a piece of paper write out each of the roles that you fulfill in your life. Then going down the list ask yourself whether your Christian faith challenges, changes, or modifies that role in your everyday living? I'm not asking you whether it should or not. I want you to look at whether your faith makes any difference in the actual living of your life. If your faith does make a difference write how underneath. For example:

father
- I try to model the love of God as the father of my children

or

student
- I pray before class silently to myself to learn more about God's truth, whatever the subject.

This exercise will help you to see what areas of your life need a greater spiritual focus.

3

Finding God at Work

For many people the idea of finding God at work is laughable. What about you? Some people would describe their work experience in more hellish terms than heavenly ones. Even if your workday is fairly pleasant most folks struggle to describe how it relates to their beliefs and personal search for God. After all, in most lines of work religion and faith aren't matters you usually talk about around the water cooler, much less in meetings or in interactions with clients. Yet the reality remains that you will spend more hours at work in your life than doing almost any other activity. Parenting by the way is also work and especially if you're the parent who stays home full-time. If the majority of our efforts, resources, and time on the planet are spent working shouldn't we consider how our employment effects our spirituality?

Work is an ancient and God given reality. Even though we sometimes day-dream about never having to work again this isn't something that God ever had on His mind. I'm sure you remember Adam and Eve who lived in the Garden of Eden. Before they ate the fruit of the forbidden tree and caused the disconnect between humanity and God to happen they had a peaceful existence in the lus-cious paradise. They were living perfect lives with the perfect God. They had everything they needed and could want right at their fingertips. They sat around and did nothing all day, right? Wrong. According to the book of Genesis Adam and Eve had a job, and that was to tend the garden and look after it's animal inhabitants. So even before the disconnect between humanity and divinity took place work was a part of the picture. Likewise, while even the great Christian teachers can only speculate about this it is unlikely that heaven is a kind of exist-ence where we will just sit around on clouds playing harps for eternity. Whatever stage or part of life we are in God has work for us to do.

Jesus in the Next Cubicle?

I'm sure I don't have to press you hard to admit the inevitably of work and it's essential role for human living. Work provides us with the means to support our families, to have shelter, and to contribute to the wider world in some small way. But how on earth are we to have a sense of God's presence in the midst of our hurried, sometimes boring and often stressful workdays? First of all, we need to remember that God is present everywhere in all places. While we can never limit God's activity or nearness to anyone place it does remain true that certain environments facilitate a better awareness of God than others. Wherever you work God is there. Remember that God is personally interested in you. God is so interested in you that He is willing to go to work with you! Depending on what it is you do for a living you may now realize how wonderful God really is! Many people bring their cell phones with them to work. At some workplaces you are not allowed to answer your cell phone during working hours, at others you are required to have a cell phone, and at many places of employment you can sneak away to answer or make a call if you like.

God is constantly calling you and always attempting to get a hold of you. The challenge is that at work, among other places, we usually keep our spiritual cell phones off. People often believe that God is somehow not welcome at work or in public life at all. If you and I were honest with each other sometimes we don't want to be bothered by God while we are doing our jobs. No matter how hostile your work environment is toward God don't believe the lie that there isn't a chance of experiencing your spiritual life at the "office", whatever form your office environment might take. Take for example this experience I had of God while working in an unusual "office" environment.

Another explosion went off as I leaned against the thick cement wall. From where I was I could see the gray sky of that chilly day through a bare opening in the building. I don't know why but in that moment I had a sense of being apart of something greater than myself. It had nothing to do with my environment, the clothes I was wearing, or what I was about to do. It was God. I think I was aware of God's presence only because I was looking for it, willing to take the time to pause in the midst of activity and focus on something else besides the immediate concerns of the moment. I moved down the line as an another explosion went off. The next guy disappeared ahead through the doorway, I was about to go next. My conscious sense of God 's closeness had to be suspended for a few moments as I darted ahead through the doorway. The Drill Sergeant yelled at me to move forward to the ditch while he proceeded to hand me a live hand grenade.

I pulled the pin, counted the appropriate number of seconds and tossed the grenade in the arching motion I was taught. It exploded and I repeated the procedure before jumping out of the ditch and back to the cement building behind the firewall.

Much of what is required to sense God's presence at work is the ability to take a step back from the immediate moment you are in. It might be as simple as taking a few deep breaths and looking out the window. It might be in marveling at how well everyone is working together and sensing that God is the midst of that unity. Much of the challenge of our workday is that we don't bother to check our spiritual cell phone messages. We don't turn the radio off for a few moments while driving from one meeting to the next. We don't bother to look up at the sky as we head from one part of the construction site to another. We allow ourselves to be totally immersed in what we are doing from start to finish. Now don't get me wrong often absolute focus and attention are required at work. Don't go closing your eyes in prayer or seeking God's active presence in your life while you're holding a live hand-grenade! The spiritual life is about balance: sometimes you need to place all of your attention on the immediate task of the moment but at other times you need to step back to focus on the great mystery of God's presence flowing through your life. So when the opportunities come to check your messages, don't just check to see if your significant other called, check to see what God is up to. On your lunch break take a couple of moments to check in with God and tell Him how your day is going. If you don't take a lunch break, figure out how to start taking one. The reality is that God is always seeking to enter the experience of your everyday life, through the circumstances, the situations, and even the people around you. So try to be a little more alert the next time you're at work, Jesus might be in the next cubicle.

Serving God Full-Time

I am always slightly bothered when I hear someone talking about "entering-full-time ministry" or when someone says my daughter is thinking about going into "the ministry." What people usually mean when they use these phrases is that someone is going to work for the institutional church in some way. Ministry is not a career. On a fundamental level, all followers of Jesus are called to full-time ministry. In fact, every follower of Jesus is called not only to full-time ministry but to a full-time life, a way of being human centered on Christ in every aspect of living.

As a parish pastor I've had the joy of seeing individuals open up their lives to God. The process of life change begins to happen and these new committed disciples tend to be enthusiastic, excited, and eager to learn and grow. Yet as they start to walk more intentionally on their spiritual journey a fear hits them. It's the same fear that I believe keeps many people from living life based on God's perspective. That fear is perhaps best personified in the comments that a woman who was growing in her faith told me, "I'm afraid what God is going to ask me to do. I mean like I am going to have to go to Africa as a missionary?" Even folks who are hesitant to accept the reality of God understand that those who follow Jesus behave and act differently, or at least that there supposed to! Much of American society is hostile to any kind of religious commitment, especially a Christian one. On the other hand there are parts of our society that see value in having a religious tradition and value system as a means to being a good citizen. The challenge for any one who seeks to follow Christ, to live their life based on the divine perspective, is that authentic spirituality is contrary to both of these views. It's acceptable to attend church weekly and have some basic moral principals you are committed to. Society can laugh at or commend this kind of commitment. The danger comes when society sees you basing all of the facets of your life on your Christian faith.

Yet, it is this total commitment to living life in Christ in your personal relationships, in your neighborhood, and at your workplace that is the defining mark of a healthy spirituality. A spiritually fit person is someone who has integrated all of the parts of his life into one unified whole immersed in the divine perspective. One of the darker parts of Christian history were the crusades. During the late Middle Ages European armies attempted to conquer portions of the Middle East, especially the Holy Land. A requirement to be a crusader and a knight was that one be a Christian. One of the marks of being a follower of Jesus is that you have been baptized by water. In a traditional baptism ceremony a person being baptized has his or her entire body submerged under the water signifying the end of their old life and the beginning of a new life based on Christ. When many of the crusaders were baptized they refused to submerge their sword arms. They knew that somehow being a Christian was inconsistent with the death that they would deal out with their swords. In my view, these individuals were not baptized at all. You can't say yes to living the spiritual life and keep your working hand above the waters of baptism.

How about you? Is there a disconnect between your attendance at weekend worship and what you do during the week? In particular, is your job something that fits into the rest of your spiritual life? Do you see your work as your ministry? Could you see it as your primary way of serving God? These are difficult questions to ask because they often lead to the fear of what God might ask us to do.

The reality is that everyone who follows Jesus is called to be a full-time mission-ary. For most of us we are called to be missionaries in our work places, schools, and local communities, not in Africa.

Is Jesus Calling You?

The historic church has a long history of emphasizing vocation and calling over career and employment mentalities. The key difference is that one is being invited by God to a *way* of life as opposed to an *activity* in life that ends after so many hours a day. Christian calling is not merely what you *do*, but it is who you *are*. Until recently the Church has tended to limit the language of calling to men and women entering the pastorate, religious life, or the priesthood, instead of proclaiming the reality that every single individual has a calling from God.

On one level every follower of Jesus receives the same call on their spiritual cell phone. It is the call to be a disciple who seeks to orient their entire life based on Christ's ways. On another level each and every follower of Jesus receives a person-alized call from God directed to their specific living out of the Christian life. The first call is always the same and always constant on a Christian's life. God will never change the voice mail He left on your soul to follow Him with everything you've got. However, it is possible from time to time that God will change your assignment, your location, or particular skill set to serve Him in a new way.

The challenge of the spiritual life is to commit yourself to living out both of these callings. The first calling is foundational; it is the relationship with Jesus that allows your spiritual cell phone to work at all. The first calling is the call to follow Jesus in every aspect of your life. If you're dialed into God and living out a healthy spirituality hearing and acting on the second specific calling will be easier. Some people have a specific calling that is constant throughout their life. They could feel called by God to practice law and bring Christ to that, they could feel called by God to paint houses and bring Christ to that, they could feel called by God to teach elementary school and bring Christ to that. For some people they don't spend their entire lives doing one kind of work. God might change their marching orders from time to time. As a believer you are called to base your edu-cation, training, and daily work patterns on the basis of how you can best serve God not on the basis of how you can best serve yourself and your career. Serving God through your employment doesn't mean you can't advance in your career but it does mean that you should consider how any potential advances would effect your ability to live life on the divine perspective.

Before moving on, I think it's important for me to acknowledge that some-times in life you have to work a job that is not in perfect alignment with the

Christian faith or your individual calling. I understand that sometimes during times of financial stress we have no choice but to be doing something that is not ideal for our spiritual health. I want to encourage any of you in such a situation to strive to make this kind of work a temporary situation in your life before it becomes the permanent story of your life. We can damage our souls if we engage in work over a long period of time that does not fit our particular calling or honor Christ.

No Retirement From Serving Christ

Jane Sellman, a commentator on woman's life once said, "The phrase 'working mother' is redundant." Just as redundant is to speak of practicing Christians. One cannot be a follower of Jesus and not let that belief spill out into every aspect of one's life. Work is a gift from God. Work as difficult as it may seem to be at times was never designed as a punishment from God. Work has always been apart of God's plan for humanity. As we go through our days at work we need to slow down, open our eyes a little wider, and take a moment here and there to check in with God. As we seek to embrace a healthy spirituality for our life we need to look at our jobs and ask the question if what we are doing is consistent with our faith.

Whatever stage of life we are in God has work for us to do. Our primary identity as individuals should be rooted in our status as a disciple of Jesus Christ. Yet, we all know that the work we do influences our sense of identify and self worth considerably. We would be wise to make sure that we anchor our employment in a divine perspective that will nourish our spirituality and not starve it. Whether we are stay at home mothers, retired, or between jobs there is never a point where we can hang up our hats and just let other people serve Christ and work for the transformation of the world. When you say yes to Jesus, you say yes to a way of life that never ends. Retirement is not a part of the spiritual journey until you pass from this world to be with God. In retirement you might slow down your workload or have greater freedom to do what you want but you should consider what God is calling you to do during this last third of your life. The truth about Christian living is that it is a calling to a full-time life that encompasses every aspect of your being. You will invest a sizable chunk of your life in spending time at work. It's critical for your spiritual health that you seek to align your employment with your spirituality.

Questions to Consider

1. Have you ever had a experience of feeling God's presence at work? Describe it.

2. What changes could you make in your attitude or schedule at work to be more alert for God moments?

3. Do you think of your job as your primary way of serving God? Why or Why Not?

4. Have you ever had a sense of God calling you to do something? If so describe it. If not, what do you think it might be like?

5. If money were not an issue, what would you want to do for work, and how would it be a means of serving God?

6. Do you find the idea of no retirement for the disciple of Jesus comforting or troubling? How do you think this concept could be played out in reality?

Exercise #1
Two Lemonade Stands: One Christ Centered the Other Not

Sit down with a group of friends over dinner or coffee and discuss what differences there would be between the operations and character of these two lemonade stands. It can be a professional, adult run business or simple, kid run business. On a flip chart or piece of paper list the possible similarities and differences.

Exercise #2
Being a Resident Missionary

Take a piece of paper and divide it into two columns. Label one column "Missionary to Africa" and the other "Missionary to X" (X being the name of your work place). First take the time to brainstorm the kind of activities a missionary to Africa might engage in. In addition, brain storm the kind of supplies and resources a missionary to Africa would need. Then attempt to transplant the activities and resources needed for Africa to being a missionary in your workplace.

For example:

MISSIONARY TO AFRICA
- Hiking Books and Safari Outfit

MISSIONARY TO XYX COMPANY
- Conservative Suit and Tie

4

Politics and Religion Do Mix

In recent years the American political landscape has been filled with considerable controversy and debate about the intersection of religion and state. It's not unusual to hear discussions of faith based values or the influence of different religious ideologies on politicians and political parties. Religion has become one part of the puzzle piece of the political game. Surely it always has been a part of the game and just as surely this approach to religion and politics does not reflect a healthy spirituality. As followers of Jesus we carry our spiritual cell phones with us at all times and in all places. We cannot pretend to ignore the voice of God speaking to us just because we are at a political event, voting, or even crafting a law if we are an elected official.

This is not to say that the Christian faith should somehow be united with the government of our nation. In fact, the worst and most horrific periods of Christian history almost all took place when the church exercised functions of the state. The church is not in the civil government business. It is in the business of telling the story of God. Moreover, the Christian faith cannot be viewed as inherently favoring one political party or group above another. Sincere followers of Jesus can be found in all of the political parities. The American Senator George Mitchell is recorded as having once quipped, "Although he's regularly asked to do so, God does not take sides in American politics." Membership in one political party or another is not a litmus test for determining who is a faithful follower of Jesus and who is not. The whole process of starting to embrace what Gandhi called "spiritual politics" is to open the door and let Jesus into your political life.

Getting Off The Bench

Many followers of Jesus are what the scholar and teacher Neil Anderson calls "secret service" Christians. In other words these are the kind of folks who are expressive about their commitment to Christ at their local church, with some of their friends, and at home with family but dare not utter a word about Jesus in

24

their public life. Their co-workers and fellow political party members have no idea of their commitment to Jesus because often their words or actions are not reflective of their faith. They haven't done the hard soul work of healthy spirituality which involves integrating all of the rooms in a human life with the color scheme of Christ. Religion has often been reduced to the observance of obligations which are nothing more than isolated events and activities. Spirituality at its best is a melody of the soul that plays freely through every aspect of your life. Therefore, the music of God's Spirit should flow through your public life so that those around you will notice that you walk to the beat of a different drummer. One time on the Fourth of July I preached a sermon entitled "Can a Christian Be Patriotic?" I remember at one of the services in which I preached this sermon I asked a rhetorical question near the beginning of my message, "Is a commitment to Christ compatible with a commitment to country?" I wasn't expecting an answer because the question was intended to get people thinking and focus their attention for the rest of the sermon. However, one individual near the front said loudly enough for most of the congregation to hear "YES!" Too often we simply assume that whatever our political views are that they are in agreement with the divine perspective. If you ever desire to become a mature person of faith you cannot leave any part of your life unexamined in relationship to Jesus. My bottom line message was that yes it is possible for a Christian to be patriotic but only based on a foundation that Jesus is Lord, not the government, not the flag, not the American dream. These are not bad things but if elevated above our commitment to God they become idols of unhealthy spirituality.

Spirituality expressing itself through politics can take many and varied shapes. There is no cookie cutter approach for Christian activity and expression in politics. For example, many evangelical and Roman Catholic Christians are active in the pro-life movement because of their spiritual commitment to God as the sole author of life and death. Likewise, there are other Christian groups that are involved in the pro-choice movement because of their own spiritual commitment that such matters of faith should not be determined by the government. Some Christians believe that under the right circumstances war is a necessary action needed to save lives or resources. Other followers of Jesus believe war is never an option that is reflective of God's love. Often as believers we share the same concerns such as fighting poverty or disease but we might disagree as to the best political strategy for achieving that end. What is important is that you don't merely accept your political beliefs and activity at face value but ask yourself the question where is Jesus leading me politically? To be honest, while certain groups of Christians are fiercely involved in the political arena, the majority are not. The

Christian faith calls for political expression. Some of us believers need to re-evaluate our methods of political activism but the majority of us need to get off the bench and get involved.

Seeking Justice on God's Terms

The Christian faith is one that calls for full expression in both private and public life. One of the difficulties of being a Christian in many cultures is that the prevailing idea of religion is that it is a private matter and should not express itself significantly in the public sector. Mahatma Gandhi the Hindu spiritual leader who led freedom movements in Africa and India expressed the relationship between politics and religion well when he said, "Those who say religion has nothing to do with politics do not know what religion is." This is not a statement that is at odds with Christian faith but rather a statement that gives expression to authentic Christian spirituality. One of the most famous verses of the Bible is Micah 6:8 which provides an excellent summary of the Bible's view of religion, "He has showed you, O man, what is good; and what does the LORD require of you but to do justice, and to love kindness, and to walk humbly with your God?" Clearly then from the divine perspective politics isn't so much an end in itself but a means to an end. In other words, healthy spirituality in the Christian faith always expresses itself in the service of others. Serving others often requires political activity because laws and the decisions of government officials have a tremendous impact on the well being of millions of people.

Most people would admit that the government has some influence on the quality of people's lives. Most people would admit that the laws of our country can help or hinder people's own attempts to improve their lives. What most people are hesitant about when it comes to politics is the idea of getting involved. Our society over the last few decades has built up a collective distrust of government and political leaders in general. For some people of faith political activity seems like a sure recipe for losing one's soul. Fierce debates, character attacks, and layers of bureaucracy seem to hinder anything good from happening in the political sphere. The key to maintaining healthy spirituality in the midst of political activity is to remember that you are seeking to serve Christ and not the agenda of a particular group or individual. As an individual believer you may not be active in every facet of politics but may take a particular interest in issues related to poverty, the environment, or human rights.

When the life of God enters into the soul of a lone individual it calls that person to work for the transformation of the world. When we step outside of the private parts of our life and into the public arena God is still talking to us. Our spiritual cell phones continue to ring. We continue to receive voice messages from God. In fact it is impossible to be a truly spiritual person if you are keeping certain aspects of your life from God. Religion in the narrow sense of the word may allow people to be Saturday night sinners and Sunday morning saints but spirituality that is holistic demands a life that is striving for authenticity at all times and in all places. Followers of Jesus are called to take part in political life not to push their agenda but to be faithful in seeking justice on God's terms. Sadly, the biggest challenge people of faith often face in the political realm is not in expressing their own views but in relating to other people who disagree with them.

Living Together with Differences

You may be aware that conversations related to politics and religion can become somewhat heated. You can take a group of friends or work colleagues who normally get along splendidly and drop a political question and you might as well have dropped a bomb. Tempers flare, people get offended, and cuts and bruises appear on the relationships between particular individuals. Remember that one of the signs of God's presence is when people get along with each other in healthy community.

One of the blessings that God brought out of that sermon I preached on the 4th of July was to encourage some people in the church who shared different political views to talk to each other. In their conversations they wanted to reaffirm to one another that at the end of day they were on the same team, not the Republican or Democratic team, but the team of Jesus Christ. One of the keys to maintaining a healthy spirituality in public life is to not lose the divine perspective. It's very easy to stop noticing God's presence and to forget that the person you are in ideological conflict with is a fellow traveler on the spiritual pilgrimage of life.

The next time you find yourself getting offended by a particular politician or individual because of their ideology or actions slow down. Take a couple of deep breaths and let God remind you deep in your soul that you and this person are far more alike than you are different. Of course you are allowed to disagree and as followers of Jesus at times we have to stand up for what we believe honors the God of love. However, as followers of the God of love we should never be accused of being non-loving to those with whom we disagree. After all, don't you and I disagree with God's perspective on a fairly regular basis? God loves us anyway despite all of the things we have done and not done.

Christian Love Can Call for Political Activity

Human beings often have the tendency to shy away from topics and discussions that might be unpleasant. You and I often choose the easy way of silence or smiling to get through tense moments in conversations. We shouldn't always confront, challenge, or correct someone but if we are going to be faithful to the presence of God in our lives we need to speak up more often. Why is it common wisdom that you don't discuss religion or politics in polite company? It's because such conversations might cause anxiety, disagreement, and controversy among the individuals in the discussion. As followers of Jesus we have to stop shying away from the hard issues of life. If followers of Jesus are truly united on the same team with God than what is preventing them from discussing some important issues about which they might disagree? If you want the color scheme of your life to match with Christ start to let the Spirit guide you politically.

Allegiance for the Christian is ultimately to the Lord Jesus Christ and not to any particular political ideology or party. Whatever your ideology don't assume automatically it is in alignment with the Christian faith. For your political beliefs and activities to be honest expressions of your spirituality you must first wrestle with Jesus about your political beliefs. You can't determine who is a faithful follower of Jesus by political party affiliation or by their view on a specific social-political issue. Social issues are greatly impacted by laws and government leadership and require a Christian response. God is always calling us and asking us to share the love He has given us with others. Sometimes love requires political activity to express itself in a faithful way.

Questions to Consider

1. What is your initial reaction to the idea of mixing religion and politics? What concerns, if any, come to your mind?

2. Do you think political views, beliefs, or party affiliation automatically indicate one's faithfulness as a Christian or not? Why or Why not?

3. In your view, is there any potential conflict between a follower of Jesus and the values, laws, and beliefs of government?

4. Do you think Christian faith requires or leads to public and political activity? Why or Why Not?

5.   What do you find the most difficult about relating to people whose political ideologies are different from yours?

6.   What is the next step for you in allowing Christ to color your politics?

Try It Out

Exercise #1
Pray Like You Preach

The Scriptures encourage followers of Jesus to pray for the government. This doesn't mean that we pray "God I'm so glad the government agrees with every-thing I believe" or "God please strike down this particular politician because I really don't like him, and I'm sure you don't either." We are called to pray for God's will to be done in the lives of our federal, state, and local government lead-ers. We should pray for wisdom in their decisions and safety for their lives and the lives of their families. We must not see prayer as a means of political lobbying for our own agenda. Yes, you should pray your conscience to Christ but you also need to be praying with sincerity for those political groups and individuals with whom you are in disagreement.

Exercise #2
Shake Hands With a Democrat (or Republican, or whatever the case may be)

Grab a cup of coffee and some sedatives, just kidding, and sit down with a fellow Christian whose political perspective is different than yours. Chat about your political ideologies and how you see them being rooted in your shared Christian faith. The point of the discussion is not to change the political perspective of the other person. The purpose of the discussion is get to know another pilgrim on the spiritual road of life. Your goal should be to let the Spirit of God show you, that despite your political differences, you are on the same team of Christ at the end of the day. Take time to pray together.

5

God's Will Be Fun?

Imagine three priests in a bar. No, this isn't some sort of bad joke but an actual experience I had not to long ago with two priest friends of mine. We had all just finished attending the annual gathering of our religious community and most of the other priests and lay brothers had already left to catch their flights to their homes across the country. Each of us wasn't due to leave till the next morning so we decided to get together for dinner. We spent several hours late into the evening sharing stories, laughing, and encouraging one other. My two friends each had a couple drinks and a cigar! It was a great time and we had a lot of fun.

Fun isn't something most people associate with Christianity or spirituality in general. I often joke that people think" if it's a miserable experience, it must be a Christian one!" Sadly, that is the perspective many people have of the Christian faith. For some of you the idea of fun and God going together is so contrary in your mind that you will struggle with the ideas presented in this chapter more so than any other chapter in the book.

I served for a time as a chaplain at a Christian camp and conference center. During the intensive months of summer with hundreds of campers and dozens of residential staff fun was always apart of what we did. I would organize ice cream parties, movie nights, and built a reputation for hiding rubber chickens in the most unusual of locations to give people a good shock. Healthy spirituality is not always about somber faces and serious conversations it is also characterized by a playfulness that comes from worshipping the God of Joy. The divine perspective encompasses life and death issues but it also encompasses the idea of enjoying the life God has given us. At my home parish, there is a little phrase painted on the door that leads into the youth room: "God's Will Be Fun." That is an accurate theological statement. If you're still wondering whether enjoying life is legal for the Christian let's consider the source of the Christian faith Himself, Jesus.

All Work and No Play Makes for Bad Spirituality

Jesus was a bar-hopper. Not in the sense that you and I sometimes think of bar-hopping because Jesus wasn't looking for romantic partner, to get drunk, or anything along those lines. He was looking to be around people, regular people, like you and me. As a traveling teacher with a growing following Jesus easily could have decided to teach and heal only in religious settings. Yet, during His earthly life Jesus almost always preferred to teach in everyday places as opposed to "churchy" places. He would meet with people at parties in their homes, in what we might call shopping plazas or malls today, and on the street corner. He met people where they worked, where they cried, and where they played. The first recorded miracle that Jesus performed was not at church but at a wedding party! That says something about Christian faith and Christian living. It's not all about misery it can and should be about celebration!

Jesus and His disciples would labor for hours or even days teaching, healing, and listening to people's problems but then they would go off by themselves for quiet prayer and rest. Christian living as often been described using the metaphor of a life long race that leads to being with God in heaven. The Christian life is a pilgrimage with Christ toward Christ. This world is not our ultimate home. Never the less our goal shouldn't be to run straight through it without stopping. God is in complete favor of you and I taking pit stops to re-charge our spiritual cell phones and reflect upon our experiences. In fact, as I often remind people especially church leaders and mothers, "Getting rest is a commandment!" In the biblical book of Genesis God creates the earth in six days and then rests on the seventh. If the God of the universe took a rest on the seventh day and has commanded that you and I are to take a rest, who are we to think we know better? All work and no play makes for an unhealthy spirituality that if left unchecked can grow toxic. Our souls are like the rich soil of a farmer's field. If you continue to work the soil season after season with no rest the soil will eventually lose it's vitality and bear little in the way of crops. Like the field our souls need to be tended, tilled, and at times left fallow so that they can rest and be restored by God's healing rain.

Enjoying Life with God

"Life sucks and then you die," is a popular expression of the perspective many people have on life. To be a follower of Jesus is not to be a person who is always smiling or giddy regardless of life's circumstances. Christian enjoyment of life is based more on contentment with where you are on the journey and less about being emotionally happy all the time. God desires that you and I enjoy the life that we have despite the ups and downs that are bound to come our way. We have to slow down and take notice of our blessings. Enjoying life with God is like enjoying life with your significant other, close friend, or spouse. During the summer months at the camp and conference center I would barely see my wife Melissa at all. I would get up early and be out by 7am and usually wouldn't get to bed till after 12 midnight. For a season intense busyness can be appropriate and won't damage your soul or your relationship to God. However, if I went for months on a schedule like that there would no marriage relationship left between my wife and I. It is the same with your spiritual life. If you continue to live life at light speed going constantly from one activity to the next, with no rest, you are doomed to become disconnected from the divine perspective. As soon as we start drifting from God, the foundation upon which our entire life rests, our relationships, work, and even our health will start to falter. It is during these toxic seasons in our life that we are most likely to start worshipping idols. Idols being anything but the one God. When we are weak we are tempted to numb our soul pain through an affair, an addiction, by eating to much or through working even longer hours.

In regard to this temptation I believe our ancestors had a distinct advantage over we who live in today's world. For thousands of years the pace of human life was dictated by the seasons of the earth. Human civilization was built upon agricultural life and so during the harvest season work would be intense but during the winter season the pace of life would slow down. Following the cycles of the earth brought human beings into a natural flow of seasons of slowness and seasons of rapidity. Jesus modeled for us the same kind of life. He would go off to the mountain to rest, pray, and relax and then He would come down from the mountain, to teach, work, and heal. Unfortunately, with the advent of modern technologies it is now possible to live life at 100mph year round.

Letting God Re-Create You

Bill Hybels the founder and Senior Pastor of Willow Creek Community Church in South Barrington, Illinois has for a number of years been very open about a period of burn out in his own life. Willow is one of the largest congregations in the Unites States with a weekend attendance of more than 20, 000 persons. I remember hearing him speak about this period in his life at a conference. One particular phrase he talked about has stuck with me and it's what a Christian Counselor said to Hybels, "I don't care what you do for recreation, but you've got to do something, you have to take the time to recreate, to let God re-create

His life in you." You and I would do well to heed the words of that counselor in our own lives. Religion is often limited to discussions about God whereas spirituality happens when a lone human being allows God to work in his or her life. Spirituality is about letting God re-create you more and more into His image. You can close the door on God. You can run through life so fast that your not giving God a chance to restore your soul, to refresh your desire for living. I'm not talking about taking a six month sabbatical or going to live in a monastery. I'm talking about learning to live your life seasonally.

If you want to be a person of spiritual maturity you must take charge of your life's schedule and find ways to balance intense busyness with quiet time. Many churches follow what is called the church year that has several seasons such as Lent and Advent. The idea of the Church calendar is to schedule life on God's drumbeat and not society's drumbeat. The Executive Director of the camp and conference center where I worked had an excellent grasp of this concept. During the season of Advent, which is basically the month of December, her family would intentionally slow down and limit their outside commitments. They would go out twice a week to the movies or to dinner and spend more time together as a family. Peggy would limit the amount of meetings she would attend during that month. During others times of the year she would be going non-stop but she understood the need for seasonal balance. That's the kind of thing you and I need to be doing. Perfect balance is of course impossible because life is messy. Yet how many of you have no seasonal diversity in your schedule at all? An annual two-week vacation doesn't count for seasonal diversity by the way! Use the church calendar, don't use the church calendar if you don't want to. But find a way that works for your living situation to live life like Jesus did. Maybe you need to finally take a lunch break. I have a friend who works in the corporate world where the standard fare is to taking a working lunch, However, he retreats to Star Bucks daily to inhale coffee and have some quiet time for spiritual reading. Walking the spiritual life is always going to put you out of step with the world's perspective but more importantly it will put you in step with the divine perspective.

Rest Now, Paint Later.

Christian living does ask us to deny ourselves at times in order to serve others and make a difference in the world. Christian living sometimes asks us to work long hours or to volunteer some of our days off for a good cause. However, every person eventually reaches that point where they no longer have anything to give. A follower of Jesus that constantly gives will quickly find that he or she no longer has anything to share. By not resting you not only endanger the health of your own soul but your ability to be a blessing to others! If you continue to use your cell phone and never stop to re-charge it what happens? It stops working, right? You and I are no different.

As Christians we are called to be artists painting the colors of grace and love over the wounds of this world. We are to be busy bending down to reach the people no one cares about and using spiritual ladders to reach those whom seem impossible to touch. Christ is the head painter, the master artist, and the one who takes our painting errors and paints over them with his own brush which is dipped in the color of royal red. There is a job to be done, which is painting the world with the color scheme of Christ. Yet as you strain and feel the aches in your back from long hours of spiritual painting remember that Jesus is telling you to take a break. Share a laugh. Enjoy good food. Notice the blessings God has given you. The season for painting will come again soon enough. Rest for now, paint later.

Questions to Consider

1. Do you think God actually desires that we have fun? Are there limits to fun from a spiritual perspective?

2. In your experience of Christianity has the message been more about activity or about the need for spiritual rest and renewal? Explain your answer.

3. How are we supposed to enjoy life with God? Can you think of any examples?

4. What kind of recreation are you engaged in? Is it the kind that brings restoration to your soul? Why or Why not?

5. Do you think the idea of living life based on seasons of busyness and seasons of rest is a viable idea? What about for you? Why or Why not?

6. What is the one step you could take right now to add more rest, quiet, or fun to your life?

Try It Out

Exercise #1
Schedule It Now!

Get your calendar out right now. Choose two months of the year where you are going to try to cut back on hours at the office and outside commitments beyond your family. For many people the months of August and December work well as months of slowness. In order to make December work you have to plan ahead of time (no shopping Christmas Eve!). Once you schedule it, defend it, and by no means change it! While your at it put in your vacation time, time for your children, and time to get away with your spouse or close friends. If you don't plan your schedule other people will do it for you!

Exercise #2
Kick Back With Jesus!

The next time you have dinner with friends make sure to include Jesus in the picture. A good way to do this is to give a toast to Jesus instead of a traditional prayer of grace, for example, "God, we are sure glad you given us great friends, great food, and great beer to enjoy! Praise the Lord!" Another way to acknowledge that we worship the God of heartfelt smiles and honest laughter is to bake a cake or other treat in honor of the Lord. Sound cheesy? Maybe it is but we need to stop separating healthy fun and rest from our spiritual lives. Healthy spirituality includes renewing times of rest as well as laughter that brings people together in community.

6

Church: More Than You Think

I was in prison. I had just walked into the visitor's room. There was a quiet assortment of folks waiting to go inside the heart of the prison to visit with a loved one, relative, or friend. As I put my personal items away in a storage locker a tough looking young man said something to the effect of "this is a————————stupid place." He was clearly frustrated. He noticed me and said with a sigh, "I'm sorry Father." I replied "Don't worry about it we're all human." He like many of the people in the room were agitated with some of the stringent rules the correctional facility required them to observe as visitors. I sat down across the room to wait for visiting hours to begin.

As we waited the young man, whom I later discovered was a truck driver, started to chat with me. We talked about his family member that was being held and his unfavorable assessment of the prison. Eventually he started a conversation about church and religion. He wanted to make something very clear, "Oh I believe, I just don't like the church thing." He talked about some of his experiences with attending church and how he didn't enjoy being hugged by strangers he didn't know. I listened with sympathy and replied, "Yeah, I'm not much of a touchy-feely person myself." I spent a little bit of time explaining the reason why church was important and he listened with interest. Eventually it was time to go inside to visit. I'm wished him God's blessings and went on my way. This sincere and bright young guy expressed the sentiment that I have heard dozens of times and I bet you have. Different people say it in their own way but essentially they are saying, "I'm a spiritual person but I'm not into organized religion."

This view is held by millions of people across the world for numerous reasons. One of the major reasons for the prevalence of this view is the lack of understanding of what Christianity, spirituality, and the church really are. Another reason is the failure of the Christian Church to model and be what God has called her to be throughout the centuries. There are many churches trapped in a narrow religion that only observes certain rituals and activities divorced from any connection to everyday living. Conversely, the Church is intended to be a place of vibrant spirituality that helps people connect to God in a personal way. Being apart of the Church is more about being dialed into the divine, embracing a new spiritual identity, and living a transformed life and less about rules, regulations, and buildings. Community spirituality, which is the true expression of the Christian faith, is never about mere institutional religion but always transcends institutions and allows the Spirit of God to transform human lives and the world.

It's Not a Place Really

I can virtually guarantee that anyone reading this sentence comes into contact with the church on a daily basis. You might not attend worship services on the weekend but you probably interact with the church all the time. It's not unusual for me to say in the middle of a sermon or a class, "True of False, the Church is a building?" and at my home congregation people are always quick to say "No, the people are the Church!." If you are a follower of Jesus then you are the Church. You don't contain the fullness or completeness of the Church within yourself but you are apart it's organic reality. I'm not talking about membership in a local church rather I'm referring to the Biblical truth that people form, express, and make up the essence of the Church. Therefore, as Christians go about their daily lives they literally bring the Church with them to work, to the grocery store, or the nightclub. Making the possibility likely that the majority of people in America encounter the Church as expressed in individual Christians on a daily basis.

Buildings only help the church to gather for worship, relational development, and other activities. Buildings are an aide to being the church but they should never become the focus of the church. When they do they become idols of unhealthy spirituality. The authentic life of the church is best captured in the collective lives of Christians throughout the ages. This encompasses not only all of the contemporary believers of our time in history, but those who have gone before us, and those who will live after us. The Church is at once present, past, and future. It along with it's Savior Jesus will last forever.

The most famous metaphor for the Church is found in the Biblical book of 1st Corinthians where Saint Paul describes the church as a body. He writes in chapter 12, "The body is a unit, though it is made up of many parts; and though all its parts are many, they form one body. So it is with Christ. For we were all baptized by one Spirit into one body—whether Jews or Greeks, slave or free, and we were all given one Spirit to drink." In other words despite what differences individuals may have related to race, employment, or religious background once they enter the Christian faith they all become apart of the one living body of Jesus

Christ. Once separate individuals they now are united together by the Spirit of God. Jesus the great cell phone tower takes the lone voices of individual spiritual cell phone users and connects them all together to form one Christian network with one united voice.

The purpose of the church, whether seen as body or network, is to tell the story of Jesus by living it and speaking it to others. It is this purpose that forms the core mission that Christians are called to accomplish in their individual lives. However, the behavior and actions of the lone Christian are never done individually because every believer through what they do and say is always giving expression to the entire Body of Christ, the Church. Healthy spirituality links the individual man or woman with the living God, but it never stops there, it always links the individual man or woman with others to form a spiritual community. Christian spirituality is never a solo performance. You and I are to play our notes and our parts as members of the Spirit led orchestra that is the Church. Christ is our conductor and we play our symphonies not in search of earthly applause but in order that others would join us in playing the melody of the Gospel. Christianity is not a me and God affair. It is always about how the individual me becomes apart of the collective we in worshipping the One God who is Trinity.

I'd Rather Golf Than Go To Church!

There is an old story that goes something like this. A mother walks into the bedroom of her son waking him up for church. The son replies, "Mom, I don't want to go to church. The people are difficult. The preaching is bad and I want to sleep in!" The mother sits on the edge of the bed gently nudging her son and says, "You have to go to church!" "But why Mom?!" the son exclaims pulling the covers over his head. "Well for starters you're 40 years old!" the mother said and "secondly you're the pastor!"

It's true that the Church is comprised of all the believers of Jesus Christ worldwide and throughout time. It's also true that there are smaller groupings of believers called congregations or local churches, several of which can be found within a few miles of where you live. Many people argue that they don't need to go to church to be a Christian. These folks say that they can worship God while they are fishing, on the golf course, or during some quiet time in their home. I know a couple who gave up on attending church and every Sunday morning dedicated time to prayer and spiritual reading with each other. It's true that you can dial into the divine perspective through all of the activities mentioned above.

I like to hike. I often have an extraordinary sense of God being very near to me while I'm walking in the woods. Being out in God's creation helps me notice the presence of the divine. However, I still attend church even when I am on vacation or away from my home parish. I know that being apart of a local community is essential for Christian living. Being connected to God is not the sole purpose of being apart of a local church. I hope you realize by now that being connected to God is the heartbeat of Christian living whether you are holding a crying baby, working late at the office, or practicing your swing at the driving range.

Being apart of a local congregation is about being connected to God through a particular group of people. Christianity can never be summed up as a Jesus and me type of religion. Christianity is always about community and it is impossible to be apart of Christian community if you are not connected to a local church. There is a Christian campfire song I learned whose chorus goes "and they will know we are Christians by our love." If your not showing up face to face with someone on a regular basis it's hard to grow in love towards them. I remember preaching a sermon about Christian community one Saturday evening and near the end of the message I made this statement, "Once you have truly experienced Christian community you will never want to go back to not having it." Several men and women nodded at my statement and then I asked those people who felt the statement was true to raise their hands. Many did.

Christian community is about being Jesus to one another. It's about giving up an afternoon to go take care of a fellow church attendee's yard that can no longer do it himself, because of a debilitating illness. This person isn't a close friend of yours but you help him out because he is are apart of your spiritual community, he is a family member in Christ. Christian community is about seeing the presence of God in the face of your fellow Christians at the birth of your child, at the death of your spouse, or at party filled with laughter. Being apart of Christian community is knowing that the *you*, who you *are*, is actually apart of the *we*, the collective we which forms the living and breathing Church.

The ancient spiritual tradition of the Way, which was one of the first names of Christianity, has always understood the very essence of God to be communal in nature. That is to say that the core identity of God is community. Christian teachers and believers throughout history have generally referred to this divine community as the Trinity: the Father, the Son, and the Holy Spirit. If healthy spirituality is something that reflects the reality of the divine perspective then to be truly human is to be apart of a spiritual community. It's true that we find authentic and life-giving community in family life and through friendships but by participation in a local church we are nurtured, sustained, and taught about the very source of community itself, who is none other than God. It is at the local church level that you can encounter God through Biblical preaching, through ancient worship practices like Holy Communion and community prayer. It is through the local church that your spiritual cell phone can be maintained, up graded, and recharged. Besides all of this how can you expect to have all of the answers, resources, gifts, and abilities to carry out the Christian mission of changing the world by yourself? You can't. Like the Anglican Priest and Poet John Donne wrote, "no man is an island," and neither you or I have what it takes by ourselves to change the world but together as the living and breathing Church we have what it takes to live Christ's mission.

Church Is A State of Being

I'd have to agree with the truck driver that I talked to in prison that I'm not much into organized religion either. If organized religion is understood to be merely a weekly event or mere rules and regulations about life. Vibrant spiritual living comes about through the alignment of every aspect of your life with the divine perspective. Being apart of a local church is one of the primary means of hearing, learning, and experiencing the divine perspective.

God has created every human being in His image but we better reflect the fullness, the likeness of God when we are together in spiritual community. In the uttermost depths of every human soul is a permanent voice mail message from God that says "you are precious, you are mine." It is only by being wired up together through the Church that you will ever be able to hear this message in it's fullness. Church is not an event but a state of being. As a follower of Jesus you express the reality of the entire Church through your own life and actions. When you cut someone off on the highway you are doing so as the Church when you take the time to help someone out in the grocery store you are doing so as the Church.

The divine drumbeat of God guides the rhythm of the spiritual hearts of all believers holding us together as one Body. The mystery of life as a Christian is the paradox of our infinite worth as a lone individual and the fact that in the great schemes of things we don't matter that much. God loves you but God loves you into community where your uniqueness as an individual finds it's true home in light of your contribution to the whole community. That's what being the Church and being apart of a local congregation are all about. If you currently aren't apart of a local church why not check out one that is just a few miles down the street? The drive might take you a few minutes but God can use a local church to bring you forward a million spiritual miles.

Questions to Consider

1. What is your reaction to the idea of "organized religion,"? Are you for it or against it and why?

2. What do you think about the idea that the majority of Americans come into contact with the Church everyday through individual Christians? Does it have any implications for Christian living?

3. If the church is really about the people do you think the focus that many congregations put on buildings and facilities is healthy? How would you place less focus on buildings and more focus on being the people of God?

4. When you consider the metaphor of the Church being the Body of Christ what comes to your mind? Do you understood this metaphor? What do you like or not like about it?

5. Why be apart of a local congregation? Did you find the discussion of Christian community helpful in seeing the importance of congregational life and participation? Or not?

6. Had you ever considered it seriously that the Church's mission is to change the world? And that you are one of the soldiers on this mission? How do you see the Church making progress in it's mission?

Try It Out

Exercise #1
The Walking and Talking Church (That's You!)

Write yourself a note and place it on the bathroom mirror, the dashboard of your car, or even as the initial greeting on your cell phone. The note should read something like "You are the walking and talking Church." Read this note before you go into work. Consider this reality as you interact with people on the street, in the office, and at school. You might be the only Church someone will ever encounter.

Exercise #2
No Buildings: Just Church

Get together with some friends and over a good meal chat about starting a church that doesn't own or rent any buildings. On a piece of paper brain storm how you would cultivate a sense of identify, where you would meet, could such a local church be a good reflection of the world-wide Body of Christ?

7

Functions of the Spiritual Cell Phone

Cell phones have the ability to send text messages, to receive voice mails, to play computer games, and to even surf the Internet. You might be the kind of person who understands every function of your cell phone or you might be the kind of person, like me, whose cell phone knowledge is mostly limited to the ability to make and receive calls. Every human being has an internal capacity to make and receive calls from God, an internal spiritual cell phone if you will. This phone has several functions to it. You and I were designed to be in communication with God on a constant basis. We have the internal wiring to live life based on divine perspective but early on in the history of humanity Adam and Eve cut the wires. Jesus re-connects us to our very selves on our soul level so that we can be in relationship to the God of Trinity. It's a gift that we have can only receive from the Divine Gift Giver, the one God. The Creator is going to give you the gift of His love, forgiveness, and relationship if you are willing to accept it. Just because you go to church three times a day doesn't mean that Christ is somehow going to love you more than your next door neighbor who watches soap operas all day.

Yet, the difference of spiritual living is that it allows us to actually experience God's love which then transforms our lives giving them meaning and purpose. We go from living in a world of black and white to living in a world of unimaginable vibrant colors. I bet you've had the experience of adjusting your sitting or standing position to get better reception on your cell phone? A couple of years ago one of the major cell phone providers ran a commercial with the reframe of "Can you hear me now?" In each commercial the cell phone user walks to a different spot hoping to get better reception and make connection with the person they are talking to. The functions of the spiritual cell phone are the ancient and time tested spiritual practices of the Christian life that help you to make the connection with God. God is always speaking to you but by positioning yourself in the right place using a spiritual practice you are far more likely to actually hear God when He speaks to you. The functions of the spiritual cell phone can be thought of as satellite dishes that give you ears to hear, eyes to see, and a heart to feel the very presence of God in your life.

The Four Letter Word of Spirituality: Pray

The well known preacher Billy Graham once wrote, "Prayer is spiritual communication between man and God, a two-way relationship in which man should not only talk to God but also listen to Him. Prayer to God is like a child's conversation with his father. It is natural for a child to ask his father for the things he needs." Prayer is a spiritual conversation between you and God. Sometimes God rings you on your spiritual cell phone and sometimes you make the call to God. Starting to pray isn't difficult. Just start with closing your eyes and focusing your attention on what is happening inside of you and say "God help me to know you more, amen." The words you use are less important than the attitude of your heart and mind. It's possible for two people to say the same exact words and conclude them with amen but for only one person to have been truly praying. There is no secret to sincere prayer other than your own desire to be in conversation with someone, namely God. If you mouth words but aren't directing them to a person that isn't a prayer. There is a great story about this that took place during the Presidency of Lyndon Johnson. Bill Moyers, who had formerly been a Baptist preacher, was an aide to the President. At a lunch gathering the President asked Moyers to lead the prayer of thanksgiving for the food. Moyers started to pray but Johnson, seated at the other end of the table, couldn't hear and said. "Speak up, Bill," to which Moyers replied, "Mister President, I wasn't talking to you."

When we pray we are talking to Jesus. We are communicating to Him the worries on our minds, the pains in our hearts, and the desires of our dreams. Prayer is the activity where you can make a difference in the world by praying for your friends, for world hunger, and the concerns of your everyday life. Spirituality is always rooted in prayer. A person walking on the spiritual path is always engaging in prayer throughout their day. Prayers don't have to be long. Anytime I hear a siren I pray a quick prayer inside my mind or quietly out loud "Lord help those in need, give courage to those who are helping." I might be stuck in traffic and starting to get uncomfortable and I'll just pray "God give me your peace!"

While you will often use words to pray don't feel that you always have to say something to God. Prayer is possible without verbal utterance. Sometimes prayer is just sitting on the back porch in the early quiet of the evening You are still and you have that sense of God's presence in the quiet of the night. That is prayer.

Prayer also involves listening. God answers our prayer through the words of other people, through the Bible, and in the quietness of our hearts. Sometimes people get verbal responses from God but generally people describe responses from God coming through an inspired idea, or a sudden clarity regarding a decision that needs to be made. Prayer happens when the active life of God is recognized, experienced, and responded to by the lone human being. Prayer is not a means by which we control God and get Him to do what we want. Prayer is the means by which we stay connected to God. Prayer is one of the primary channels by which God can give you nutrients for your soul. If you starve yourself of prayer, you are literally starving your soul. The best way to start becoming a person of prayer, is to start to pray. Start slowly and grow as you go. Prayer forms the foundation of the Christian life. In fact the four letter word of spirituality in almost every world religion is spelled p-r-a-y. So get praying!

The Divine Perspective in Print

Recently I heard an alarming statistic regarding the reading habits of Americans. The average American reads only one book every year! One book. I doubt that in the majority of cases it's the "good book." The Christian Church throughout the centuries has always understood the Bible to be the primary means by which God communicates His divine perspective to people. The Bible is the written account of God's relationship with certain people through history. The Bible was not written as a science textbook, a self-help book, or a guide on how to be a prosperous person. The Bible is fundamentally a book on understanding how relationships work. The principal relationship the Bible focuses on is the relationship between God and humanity. The second major focus of the Bible is how you and I are to treat each other as fellow beings made in the image of God. Remember relationships, human and divine, are the meat and drink of life. The Holy Scriptures gives us the divine perspective on human living. The challenge for most of us is that we have grown up in a culture and society that is not based on the divine perspective. Spiritual living involves a great deal of letting the Spirit of God transform your understanding of the world. The goal is to shift the center of your worldview from the human perspective to the divine perspective. I like to it call it putting on the "Jesus glasses." If you and I are to participate in the great mission of painting the world in the color scheme of Christ it is crucial that we first see the world as Christ does. The Holy Scriptures provides you an opportunity to see the world from the perspective of God. The Bible is our gateway to the wild depths of spiritual truth. Reading and understanding the Bible like other functions of the spiritual cell phone can and should be done individually, but are best practiced within the context of Christian community. This is where the local church comes into play. The Spirit of God works through the stories, poems, and historical accounts of the Bible to connect us to Him. The Bible was written by a community of persons and meant to be understood within a community of persons. That community is the Church. Jesus is the chief personality and superstar of the Bible. For the follower of Christ the great storyline of the Bible always connects to the Savior. The Scriptures gives us access to the divine perspective in readable print! To know the Bible, the Word of God, is know the Word of God, the person, Jesus.

Worshiping in Community

The entire life of a follower of Jesus is intended to be an act of worship. Worship is how we proclaim to the world who is our master, who is our joy, who is the ultimate priority of our lives. However, in narrower sense worship is what happens when you gather together with others at a local church service. Different Christian traditions carry out worship in different ways ranging from highly structured prayers and poetic rituals to casual settings of upbeat music and spontaneous prayer. The purpose of these worship services is connect people to God in community. The end result of a worship service should be to plug the lone believer of Christ into the divine party where together with all believers, across time and space, God is celebrated. A worship service should help you experience a place in your soul that is different from the everyday experience of your life. Whether you attend Mass at a Roman Catholic Church or a praise and worship service at a non-denominational church you should be seeking to encounter God through community worship. It is only within the context of community worship that ancient spiritual practices like Baptism and Holy Communion can take place. Baptism and Holy Communion are what the church has traditionally called sacraments, or ordinances, which according to the classic definition are "outward and visible signs of an inward and spiritual grace." I'd like for you to think of the sacraments as sacred gateways to Christ. For centuries people have met and encounter the Holy God through these practices. They don't work robotically but if you approach them with a desire to touch the divine, God will be there for you. In addition, to the sacraments we have the opportunity to encounter God through the preaching of the Holy Scriptures. Through God's servant, the preacher, God speaks His love letters to God's people. One of the mysteries of Spirit inspired preaching is that there can be 500 people in the congregation but it seems like the preacher is speaking directly to you. That's not a clever preacher, that's a clever God at work in your life! Your spiritual cell phone can never be fully re-charged, or be fully functional if it doesn't get regularly plugged into community worship.

Don't Just Sit There and Be Holy. Do Something!

Being spiritual involves more than attending worship services, reading the Bible, and praying. Being the church, for you are the church, is participating in Christ's mission to transform the world. A spirituality that hordes wisdom, joy, and the knowledge of God for itself is a bankrupt spirituality. Authentic spirituality always seeks to share wisdom, to give joy, and to spread knowledge of God with reckless abandon. Serving others is the heartbeat of Christian spirituality. Serving others doesn't always require that you become a missionary in Africa but it does require you be a missionary in your neighborhood, at your job, and in your wider community. It's important to remember how Jesus envisioned His church, His community of hope givers, to function throughout the centuries. After Jesus was resurrected from the dead He spent forty days with members of the early Christian community. At the end of these forty days Jesus gave His last earthly words to His disciples before returning to God the Father. He gave them what I guess you might call the mission statement of Christianity, in Church circles it's called the Great Commission.

"Then the eleven disciples went to Galilee, to the mountain where Jesus had told them to go. When they saw him, they worshipped him, but some doubted. Then Jesus came to them and said, "All authority in heaven and on earth has been given to me. Therefore go and make disciples of all nations, baptizing them in the Father, and of the Son, and of the Holy Spirit, and teaching them to obey everything I have commanded you. And surely I am with you always, to the very end of the age (Matthew 28:18-20)."

Jesus didn't tell His first disciples to "Therefore go and spend all of your time attending church activities like worship services, small groups, and meetings." The mission is to go out into the world and make a difference. One of the greatest temptations of Christian life is to get trapped into the "Holy Huddle" syndrome. The Holy Huddle happens when Christians get content hanging out at church and with each other to the point of ignoring the wider world.. Jesus didn't sit around in church all day speculating about theology or enjoying the company of His friends. He went out into the messy world and made an impact on people's lives. So don't get stuck in a spiritual armchair. Healthy spirituality always leads to action.

Spirituality Is For Everyone!

Sometimes we make the mistake of thinking that authentic and vibrant spiritual living is only available to a select few people. We think that real spirituality is for the monk, the priest, or the brilliant scholar. Nothing could be further from the truth. If it were why did Jesus choose regular men and women, with regular jobs, with houses and kids to be His students. Why didn't He choose the great minds, the religion teachers, or the temple priests to be apart of His inner circle? I think I know why. To make it clear once and for all that God is deeply interested in each and every person, including you! The functions of your spiritual cell phone provide time-tested pathways through which you can encounter God. You can grow to be more faithful in prayer or more understanding of God's perspective through Scripture. You can learn to dial into God on a deeper level through worship and you can learn to serve others with greater compassion and frequency. Spirituality is not rocket science and for that I am deeply grateful because the wonderful thing about living life according to the divine perspective is that everyone is invited to join in! There are literally thousands of resources on growing in prayer, understanding the Bible, learning to worship more intentionally, as well as how to serve others in Christ's name. Start pushing the buttons of your spiritual cell phone to let God know you are interested in experiencing Him on a deeper level. The surprise of spirituality is that just as we reach to press the "talk" button on our spiritual cell phone God is already there talking to us.

Questions to Consider

1. What has been your experience of prayer in your life? Do you remember when you were first exposed to the concept of prayer?

2. If prayer isn't about "getting what we want from God" then what is it about?

3. Have you ever considered reading the Bible as a way to encounter God? Why or Why not?

4. What is your view of the purpose of a worship service? Have you ever experienced God through a worship service? If you have, what was it like?

5. How do you balance prayer, worship, and the study of Scripture with action? Can you?

6. Do you think real spiritual living is really accessible to regular people? Why or Why not? How would it work for someone like you?

Try It Out

Exercise #1
Prayer Prompts

Prayer shouldn't be limited to one period of the day for the follower of Christ. However until prayer becomes a healthy habit we can be so busy in our lives that we go through an entire day without praying. An easy way to start soaking your day in prayer is by developing what I call prayer prompts. A prayer prompt is anything that can remind you or cue you to the necessity of praying. When you encounter a prayer prompt you then immediately pray. It can be a short prayer inside of your heart or said quietly aloud.

Here are some examples of prayer prompts and prayer responses I've used in my own life:;

- Ambulance/Police Sirens "God help those in need, give courage to those who are helping"
- News Report of Deaths "God give peace to their souls, comfort those who mourn"
- An Upset Person "Lord, I don't know what is troubling *Joe*, but give *him* your peace."

Almost anything can be a prayer prompt, choose a couple for your own life and go from there.

Exercise #2
Increasing your Biblical Diet

Many Christians desire to understand the Bible with greater clarity and to read the Bible with more regularity. Despite this desire many followers of Jesus never get into the Bible on their own. Here is a list of suggestions to help you start reading and understanding the Bible on a regular basis:

- Buy a Bible with a newer translation like the New International Version or the New Living Translation.

- Join a Bible study at your local church. If there isn't one ask the pastor or priest to start one!

- Join a Bible study at another church.

- Join an Online Bible study. They do exist! I lead one for example.

- Start Reading the Gospel of Mark. It's the shortest Gospel and will give you a basic overview of Jesus' life.

- Don't read for distance. Read for understanding.

- Better to read with focus for 5 minutes than to read several chapters quickly in 50 minutes.

- Use a daily devotional that gives you bite sized sections of Scripture to read everyday.

8

Maintaining Your Signal

When I was studying theology and history in college I was also serving on the staff of a local church. This was also the first year of my novitiate, the initial training period for members of my religious community. If all of that wasn't enough I worked a part-time job in the dead of the night as a security guard. It helped pay for my studies and the roof over my head. One of the places where I did security work was a high-end spa and hotel facility that mostly catered to the corporate world. The basic job of the security guard is make your rounds, make sure everything is quiet and calm, and to lock up and open up doors. I had a walkie-talkie but the most important piece of equipment I had were my keys. I had dozens of keys on a single key ring. I had keys to the gym, the health spa, the office, and numerous other buildings on site. One time in the early morning hours I went to use the bathroom. There was no one around. Just me. I went into the stall and took care of my business. I stood up and pressed the lever for the toilet to flush. At the exact moment that I pressed that lever the keys fell off my belt and directly into the toilet. They were flushed away in a matter of seconds! I stood there in shock. I couldn't believe what had just happened. What was I to do?

In a few hours I was supposed to unlock everything. I left the bathroom and paced around the building trying to think of a way to get out of this situation. I was stuck. Then in desperation I made my way to the maintenance area and found the third shift maintenance guy listening to music in the workroom. I felt awkward and already embarrassed before I said anything to him. I almost didn't saying anything but I really didn't have any choice. I blurted out, "Yeah hi, I um, flushed the keys down the toilet." His immediate reaction was to laugh. He thought my joke was pretty funny. The trouble was I wasn't joking. I repeated myself a little more firmly "No, really I flushed the keys down the toilet." The guy laughed again but noticing the expression on my face began to laugh so hard I thought he was going to explode. I had to tell him my embarrassing story and then he gave me an extra set of keys. I was off the hook but I certainly wasn't expecting that to happen!

As you make your rounds through life things will happen that you didn't expect to happen. Your best friend turns against you, your child gets deathly sick, or you lose your job. In retrospect, my situation with the keys was humorous but to often the garbage that life throws at you isn't funny at all, it's heartbreaking. When life goes down hill it can seem like you are cut off from God. The former connection you experienced with the divine perspective seems to be nothing more than a pale memory. You and I often experience major reception problems in our spiritual life when suffering, tragedy, and pain come our way.

What Gives with a Loving God and a Suffering World?

Roman Catholic Priest and Franciscan Richard Rohr says that "Spirituality is always about what you do with your pain." The question that every generation of human beings is destined to wrestle with, is "why pain at all?" If the divine perspective of God is fundamentally about love, transformation, and personal relationship that why do we have a world filled with the opposite of these things? If the Bible is correct in saying that "God is Love," what gives with a largely loveless world? These are classic questions of human existence and you would do well to ponder and pray over them. To grow as a spiritual person you must wrestle with the question of suffering and how you will approach suffering in your own life. The Bible, which gives us the divine perspective in print, provides us with some explanation as to why our world is so messed up. As you will recall God's original idea was for humanity and divinity to live in perfect harmony in the Garden of Eden. Unfortunately, Adam and Eve pulled the plug on that harmony and caused a rift to occur between people and God. Sin, that which separates us from God and our true selves, entered the world. According to the Christian story on life the disconnect that took place wasn't only between human beings and God, the disconnect that took place was between *all* of creation and God. The very planet, the solar system and the ecosystems of our world were disconnected from the leadership of the Holy God. Therefore, in a fallen world not in alignment with its Creator natural disasters, awful diseases, and all kinds of evil can and will take place.

God does not sit up in the heavens with the heavenly host and push buttons to inflict diseases and tragedy on people. Life is not a cosmic reality TV show where the angels vote who to punish next with God gleefully agreeing to their vote. The world is in rebellion against God. Hand in hand with this notion of a fallen world is the concept of free will. If God were to create a being that was truly in His image, it would have to have free will, the ability to make our own choices. We aren't robots. Individual human beings can choose to follow God or not. One of the greatest gifts God has given humanity is the freedom to do what we want to do in our lives. This freedom has always been humanity's greatest gift and greatest curse. It is with free will that we can choose to feed the hungry or choose to drop a nuclear bomb. Freedom in the Biblical sense comes at a great cost.

God Guides Us Through the Storm

Yet, the pain that you experience in this life doesn't have to be pointless. The mystery of the Christian faith is that God can take the worst circumstance and bring something good out of it. Christian spirituality is fundamentally a realistic spirituality. By that I mean that Christian faith acknowledges that life is difficult, it's painful, and not always pretty. There is no promise from the divine perspective that if you walk with God your life will be free of pain. The promise is that you will never have to the face the pain alone. Utter darkness cannot consume you. Even if the shadows of depression and difficulty surround your soul Jesus will be there with you, holding a light to keep the darkness at bay. The promise of Christian living is not that God will always deliver you from pain but that God will get you through the pain to new life.

When I was in high school I spent one summer working as a counselor at a Christian summer camp. We had several hundred campers and staff living on site for a week at a time. I remember one evening a terrible storm rolled in. There was lighting, fierce winds, and much to the shock and fright of many of us a Tornado warning. This was New England, none of us were use to this sort of thing! Many of the kids we had at the country camp were from the city and so the prospect of facing a storm like this out in the woods terrified them. The entire camp came together to hunker down in the basement of the kitchen facility. It wasn't long before many of the children were tearing up and getting panicked. The rain poured, the wind smacked its way across the building. The noises were unfamiliar to many of the staff and the kids. Tough teenagers from the inner city were crying and trying to find their younger siblings. Even a few of the staff lost their composure. Finally some of us began to sing. We sang songs that gave praise to God. We gathered all of the kids together, we held hands, we prayed. We stayed connected to God despite reception problems. Eventually the storm past with no Tornado touching down in our area. We returned to our cabins for a shaky night of sleep. God got us through the storm, but God didn't take the storm away. Such is the way that God often works in your life and mine. Besides getting us through the storm God used that storm to grow the friendships and trust levels among our campers and staff. We were a stronger community after the storm than we had been before the storm. My cabin of 10-year-old boys came together in a way that was remarkable considering how they had previously delighted in kicking, attacking, and fighting with each other. God does work miracles in the face of difficult circumstances! The reality is that success doesn't teach us that much in life. Most of our growth as human beings comes out of our experiences of failure and tragedy. The promise of God is that He won't leave you in tragedy if you keep talking on your spiritual cell phone. They key is to not hang up when the going gets rough.

Jesus: What a Loser!

As you probably know Jesus was unjustly accused of several crimes and sentenced to death. He was nailed to a cross and endured hours of physical torment before dying. The great movement that Jesus had begun seemed to come to a crashing halt. Many of Jesus' friends and students went into hiding. Eventually many of them went back to their old jobs, to their former way of life. It seemed like Jesus started out His public life a winner but ended it as a loser. The traveling teacher who taught about a God that ordinary people could connect to now seemed disconnected from that God. He was dead. Many historians and thinkers have labeled Jesus as a loser. Others have proposed that Jesus never intended to go die on a cross. It was all random chance. They say it demonstrated Jesus' lack of leadership and vision in realizing what His opponents were capable of.

Personally I think those kinds of folks are missing the entire point of Jesus' life and death. It's not surprising that many people miss the point of Christ's death on the cross. It makes no sense from the human perspective. Success is about winning. From a worldly perspective God should be the ultimate winner. God's got all the power, all the resources, and all the authority to do what He wants. Why in the world would God want to lose?

The great mystery of spirituality is that to the way to win, is to lose. As human beings each of us is broken deep down inside. Our souls have been unplugged from their homeland, which is God. In the past people believed God favored the successful, the powerful, and the brilliant. Jesus' death on the cross crushed that lie forever. Can you imagine a God that would take the place of the loser to show that all of us can be winners in His love? That's the kind of God that the Christian faith proclaims. Instead of staying safe in heaven from the pains that human beings inflict upon one another, Christ came and took them upon Himself. The cross of Christ shows us that God is capable of taking any amount pain and transforming it into a blessing. Christ is always working as the Holy Mid-Wife to take the painful labors in your life and to birth blessings out of them. Before you and I can be resurrected, that is transformed by God's love, we must first experience the crucifixion. We must lose to win. Our God said, "hey I'll be the loser so that you be the winner for eternity."

Let's Go Through This Together!

It's important to realize that God does not delight in your suffering. God is always after you, not to punish you, but to love you! The divine perspective of God is at odds with the perspective of the fallen world. You and I have the choice to live our lives on the basis of our own perspective or the divine perspective. God will not force Himself upon us. When life gets rough it's crucial that we continue to stay connected to Christian community so that others can help us. When black clouds settle over your soul they can rob you of your spiritual motivation. You can feel no desire to press the buttons on your spiritual cell phone, to engage in spiritual practices, or to reach out for the helping hand that Jesus is offering. The community of faith helps us when we can't help ourselves. We might not have the energy to pray but people will pray with us. We might not have any idea what section of the Bible to read but someone gives us a passage to look at. Just as God promises to never leave us or forsake us such is the promise of authentic Christian community.

God is not in favor of suffering for the sake of suffering. Despite popular belief suffering is not inherently a means of "building character." Suffering can warp the image of God in a human soul by taking away its inherent dignity. Suffering can lead people to acts of desperation that betray their own beliefs. The wonder of Christ's act of love in dying on the Cross reveals us to that even death, pain, and suffering are not the final words in this life. Nor are they truly capable of blocking our connection to God. Our reception might get fuzzy during the dark days of our life. Yet, if we keep talking to God on our spiritual cell phone our faith will stay intact and surprise of surprise we may yet get a better signal than we did before.

God who is the Master Playwright of the Universe can take the worst turn of plot and transform it into a happier ending. Life seldom gives you the part you want to play. While God will get you through to the next scene, it may not be according to the storyline that you had wanted. The next time you flush your keys down the toilet or the next time trial and tribulation come your way don't be afraid to share your situation with Christ. Unlike the maintenance guy who laughed at me Christ will hold your hand, look you in the eye and say "I know your pain, I'm crying with you, let's get through this together."

Questions to Consider

1. In your own life, are you still surprised at suffering and pain when they come your way? Why or Why not?

2. Have you wrestled with the concept of suffering and a loving God? What are your thoughts about this topic? Can the two ideas, of suffering, and a loving God be reconciled? Why or Why not?

3. What is your response to the idea that the entire creation, the entire planet, is fallen? Does that help you to understand the world or not? Why or Why not?

4. Do you believe that human beings actually have free will? Do you find this idea at all helpful in understanding the suffering in the world? Why or Why not?

5. Has God every helped you to get through a difficult period in your life? How so?

6. How have you understood Jesus' life, death, and resurrection in the past? Did this chapter challenge or confirm any of your thinking? How so?

Try It Out

Exercise #1
Let God Have It!

Often when tragedy comes our way we are left confused about the nature of God's love. We have questions, we feel doubts, and very often we feel angry with God. My advice to you when you're going through a dark time is to let God have it. Tell Him *exactly* how you feel. Shout. Cry. Be Angry! God's desire is that you come clean with Him. It might be helpful for you to have a focal point for this very emotional and visceral type of prayer exercise. You might want to look at a painting of Jesus or an Icon of Jesus. Whatever it takes to help you be direct and honest with the Lord, go for it.

God is not ashamed of our feelings. Quite the contrary, God wants to comfort us, and to be with us in the midst of our pain. We have to be real with God and give Him all of our pain, even our pain concerning Him.

Exercise #2
The Timeless Debate: Suffering and God's Love

Get together with a group of friends. Divide the group into two teams. One team will argue the case that suffering proves the point that God is not loving. The other team will argue the case that God is loving despite the suffering in our world. Keep track of major arguments and points on a flip chart or a large piece of paper. After the debate share a meal and discuss as a group the merits of each perspective and what your personal view is of the topic.

Conclusion

My initial reaction to going to church when I was a kid wasn't a pleasant one. My father is an atheist and during my early years it was just my father and I living together in a little country home. When my father married the woman whom I consider to be my mother the expectations about Sunday morning suddenly changed. I was now required to go to church! I didn't care much for it. Eventually it got better as I made friends and started to get involved in some of the activities of our local church. In my early teenage years I was once again at odds with the Church. I enjoyed the social component but felt like Christianity didn't have any spiritual depth. I have always wanted to desperately know and experience the divine. So in my hungry quest for God I experimented with new age spirituality and eastern religions. It seemed to me at the time that these approaches to life actually considered the experience of the divine very important. My experience with the Church had not stressed a living and breathing relationship with God. From my teenage point of view the local church I was a part of stressed community, good values, and helping others. All good things but I wanted to *know* God, not just know some facts *about* Him.

Thanks to God working through the prayers of some friends I gradually started to explore the rich treasury of works on Christian spirituality from centuries long past and the present day. I discovered there was profound meaning and truth behind the basic claims of Christianity. I had made a profession of faith that I believed in Jesus Christ as my Lord during the course of my church life as a young person. What God did was to finally connect that profession of faith with the entirely of my life. The Spirit of God was finally helping me see that what I prayed, sung, and did on Sunday morning had profound implications for how I lived out every other aspect of my life. My spiritual cell phone, which I had occasionally used, suddenly came to life with voice messages from God, with prayers, and a desire to connect all of my life with the heartbeat of Christ. Your own spiritual cell phone may have been active for years but it is my hope that this little book has helped you to connect your faith to every aspect of your life in a deeper way.

Lively spirituality that honors God and transforms your life is based on the truth that all has the potential to be sacred. It's God's world after all and so no matter where you go there is the opportunity to be connected with Him. The hard work of spiritual living is in aligning every department of your life with the divine perspective. Religion as it is often understood settles for a discount God and a discount spirituality that do no affect your life beyond attendance at worship. Authentic religion and spirituality overwhelm your soul with the music of the Heavenly Maestro so that your life cannot help but dance according to Christ's ways.

Christian faith requires that you say yes to the mission of changing the world, resisting dark forces, and overcoming evil. When you say yes to Jesus Christ you are saying yes to be a full-time secret agent for the Kingdom of God. Being a Christian brings real drama and action to your life! In the movie of everyday living Jesus Christ is the superstar but you and I get to play exciting supporting roles. The plots are infinite. The characters are colorful and the consequences eternal. So my challenge for you is to stop sitting on the bench of spiritual sloth. Sign up for an adventure. Start pushing the buttons on your spiritual cell phone. God is waiting for you!

978-0-595-37321-5
0-595-37321-6

Printed in the United States
39752LVS00006B/160-204